Printed in Canada

First Printing, 2019

ISBN 978-1988959-01-6

Rosenna Imprints
13 Veterans Dr.
Lewisporte, NL
A0G 3A0

Cover design by Soap Designs Inc.

<u>Dedication:</u>

This

Is for

The Cherry Blossom

And

The Ostrya

As Light

Cast dimly on an empty stage
Growing fainter in a spoken phrase
Although the timely numbers grow and gage
Words spoken in a drunken haze.

Unlike the brilliant light
That stoops to stare and watch
This glow keeps memories out of sight
Hoping swiftly, cowardly not to botch.

As friends help to pull and stretch
Dim fog resists and holds its ground
It's only hope has come to catch
The last remains of its soft sound.

Stage lights fade to black
And friends return into the now
A hopeless dream not coming back
The play ends, take one final bow.

Shadows Of Light

With life
There is dark
Stormy acres of hate
With scattered chance
Of sadness
Plus, an added bonus
Of never-ending
Desperation.

With the dark
There are shadows
Unseen by most
Only seen
When one sees
Themselves
As they are shadows
Only bound
When the sun falls to her knees
And the dark
Overwhelms.

With the shadows
There is hope.
Cowardly praise
For the time
Wasted away.
Heaven's chaos
In circles
Like unknown life
Peering through a screen
Understanding us better
Than we comprehend
Ourselves.

<u>With Every Night</u>

With every night
You fade from your life
Taking my hopes,
My soul,
My light
And hold it tight
Within your grasp.

With every dawn,
You steal my passion
And drag it across
A perfect blue sky
With crying words
Yelled swiftly high.

With every time
You say goodbye
You reach a hand
Into my heart
And pull out
The imperative part.

Your Photo In My Wallet

I kept your photograph,
the one from a million years ago,
and tucked it away
inside my wallet,
below my library card
from lives come and gone,
and above my ID,
that doesn't look like me anymore.

I kept the photo you gave me,
long into knowing you.
Through storms, and sun
you remained only slightly tattered
beneath my cracked library card
and above the old and long haired me.

I kept the photo in my wallet
even after we drifted apart
for even though
you won't spare me a glance
this photograph is memories
so, tucked away it will stay
forever.

I kept your photograph,
now I am long gone and forgotten.
years have gone by without a thought
it's quiet.
and though it's not next to me,
if you look you will see
I kept that photograph of you
within my wallet sleeves
tucked away
beneath the new library card
I got before I left
and above a new photograph
which replaced an ID
which never looked like me.

With Love,

The slippery soul
Of ocean rain frolics.
Quiet Mountains of war
Juggle light.
The dark smoke chaos,
During winter storms,
The Earth's crashing sky,
The sharp air.
Delirious souls declaring
Contented Murder.

In A Dream

a knife and bullets
aimed at my head
ghostly limbs hold handles and
triggers
as airplanes choreograph
swiftly above my bed.

empty bullet holes and
stab wounds
leave feeling of numb
but pain reaches my bloodstream
like small needles
injecting confusion
and raw emotions.

awake now I lie
and feelings remain
unable to trace the
source of the detached pain
live through life
shadowed by unreal feelings
until I dream
again.

Ephemeral

And tiny hands reach
Towards an end
Upon the horizon
Laid empty with
Angelic haze.

With beating hearts
The children march
Black holes for souls
And the abyss
for spare parts.

Each day brings life
A shorter rope
And pulls it close to hand
Volatile fists hold them near
As Life and Death elope.

Lips press tight
And chasms shift and whirl
She a takes a look up at the sky
Nothing more could be said
By the ephemeral girl.

Hypnic Jerks

land stretches lazy arms
standing tall, you watch over.
life passes around you.
a carousel ride.
the void urges you
stepping closer
almost hanging off the edge
too close for comfort
l'appel du vide,
you are curious
what would happen
if you were to
jump.
it hits you
you jolt awake
blood pumping
heart speeding
sweating
you fall back
head hitting comfort.
it wasn't real.

A Town To Not Call Home

Living in this town,
Cannot be called my home
No room for me
Nothing of my own.
Impressions tarnished
And how things used to be
Though people invited
A feeling, melancholy.
An ache burns
Reminiscent thoughts collide
Voices sear my ears
Memories I do not share.
The harmony subsides,
Locked in this place
My shape doesn't fit the hole,
Watching the world move without me
Through a sky,
Deep as charcoal.

A Pulse

A soft beating
Lulling my numbed soul
Rhythmic and living.
Quiet fingers search the veins
Pressing deep into skin
Slowly losing my breath,
Though anxiety falls
Soft beats of a drum
A reminder of life.
Under a thin layer of flesh
A life force pumps
Fuel like a car
All worries float away
As my fingers sense
And calm down to
The beat of my thriving pulse.

<u>Colours</u>

Lemons and tarts
Soft chickadees sing.
Lip Balm and pineapples
While bumble bees sting.
Scrunched up faces
A laced and dotted box.
Cats glowing eyes
And children's playtime blocks.

Touch gets sharper,
Clouds burn in almost fire.
Sunrises bloom like tiger lilies
It rolls off the tongue of the liar.
Juice squeezes into a glass
And like sand it burns your feet.
A childhood toy sits on a shelf
It's wiped from the brow of the athlete.

Poison leaks from a skull capped vial
Blood drips down the chin of a lion.
Tulips bloom in burning sun
It blows away the innocent dandelion.
A house crumbles around ashes
Spite fuels a motorcycle across tarmac.
Knives cut and spill
Flashing before it fades to black.

Coffee Stains On Coat Sleeves

I watched you sitting by yourself
And wished I could reach out.
With every moment
That passed by
I noticed something new.

Thing never seen before
Lungs and eyelids became sore
With everything
I didn't know
My entire soul collapsed.

A straw held between your teeth
You looked nervously around.
A useless mouth, wiped
Across your sleeve
Then everything made sense.

And what you seemed to do
Was done by someone else
For that coffee stain
On your coat sleeve
Appeared on mine as well.

A Random Stanza

And though I speak in broken form
Our star-crossed hearts will soon be shown
When the "Us" becomes an "I"
Our lives continue to the sky.

The Shadows Kill

A twisted hand
That grows inside
Ripping ideas
And emotions alike

Tear stained paper
Traced in ink
While shaking hands
Urge thoughts to unthink

A claw marked casket
Buried alive
Six feet under
Hidden, yet unable to hide

The hand that grows
Reaches towards
And though pure hands
Grasp and pull
They must be reminded:
The Shadows Kill

<u>Rose</u>

A rose bush
With a single rose
Is not the same as
Twenty.
But placing petals
Perfectly
Can feel like just as many.

And if a rose is
Plucked from the bush
It gains a bit of value
Until the rose
Decides to die
And withers
Into darkness.

But a rose bush
Left to its own
May not survive
The night
And so the bush
Resigns to a life
With nothing good in sight.

Cafeteria Seating is Restricted to 50 Persons

I wish the world would pause
And time would cease to move.
I wish to be released from the cell
Holding the spirit in the tomb.

I wish you could see the subtle twitch of thumb
And hope the same as me.
I wish you felt this hole inside
The slow abyss of a fated love.

And every time I make a wish
I feel your presence there
Telling me you love me too
And guiding me to the air.

Draped In Darkness

The contrast between light and dark
Is something to be desired
As having only light is hard
But the dark destroys the tired.

With a life full to the brim
Of an abyss draped in dark
Something in you makes me smile
And out flies a shining lark.

So, with a fleeting hand I throw
The morning glory to your heart
With open arms I hope for you
To bring us both back to the start.

Time

The clicking of the passing time
Thoughts and ideas written in rhyme
While eyes and souls fade by nine
Each ticking sound a neon sign.

The unending end of seconds passed
A hand of God has been cast
Unto the world with face aghast
Only sails lifted to higher mast.

So now I stare up to the sky
And see the clouds as time gone by
Let's leave our souls and minds behind,
Forget that time has made us blind
And say goodbye to us who've died.

A Shooting Star

I wish I didn't feel like this,
with every push and shove.
I wish I could just move ahead
and arrive at tomorrow's dawn.

I wish you could see the half of it
and understood the fear
I wish the thoughts were left behind
And that you were safe and near

But everything I do collapses
and my person becomes a void.
I feel the warmth removed from my heart
leaving the call of death behind

I wish I could put into words
how I don't know what to say
and I wish that you could pull me through,
I could live to see another day.

but wishes never granted
leave the broken ones forlorn
so I will sit here waiting for
a single shooting star.

Storms and Paths and Lives

The silence aches
like storms abroad
and I feel as though emotions passed
through metal now turned plastic rods
feed into fear
sending lightning strikes
between broken people
whose minds alike
no longer hear the beaten path
or storms clouds rumbling overhead
but look to each other
with hope they said
"A life turned blind
Is one life bled."

<u>May 7th 2018</u>

So stop the world
and watch it fall
I don't want to be here
anymore
and I hope you find some
peace
in the life you stole
from
me

<u>12:30</u>

And failing hands reach out
for light
in hopes to end
the black
but bright when meeting dark
turns grey
so we live in slight sorrow
for another day

<u>Coping</u>

an endless hallway
spiraled in dark
but the end is right there
and the end is nowhere

so demons and monsters
alive in my head
get trapped behind layers
of metaphorical cement

but they're never quite gone
just dormant for now
though you promise me that
the doors keep them out.

though it's hard to believe
i understand the thought
this metaphor works
to cope with the what.

When Writing

Pages torn in pieces
Leave words a broken thought
But keeping them in cages
Is something I wish not

Though words left to
Wander free
Find solace in the dead
So traveling words
Can find no peace
Where you cannot find dread.

Constellations And The Night Sky

And stars
Gathered in broken
Clusters
Never heal one another
But rather feel
Less alone
In a universe full of
Perfect constellations
So the stars
With higher built up weight
Burn up and die
The quickest
Now the stars in
The broken clusters
Are falling from the heavens
Leaving a
Perfect sky
And perfect stars
To keep the world
From darkness.

The Handmade Calendar

Like broken words
And phone screens blurred
Things are said that sound absurd
Though nothing can be overheard.

I feel like thoughts thrown
Canceled by headphones
Leave more than one feeling alone
In unmeaning ways, unthoughtful tone.

So, science tests
Lead fearsome quests
Near ideas to be expressed,
Time invests
And manifests
The power to do the rest.

And It's Okay

I watch as
the words flutter
from broken skies
and hope that clouds
move over fast
so stars once blocked
can breathe again
for we are one
who share
a life
and it's okay
we'll live again.

For Me

cascading whirlpools
in polyester lives
grip the comfort of
angered seas
as they wash towards
an ink-drawn shore
of lying breaths
and hopeless
help
watching candles burn
and blown out
in one last
tranquil sigh.

<u>Foam Soap</u>

Hold the
hands of
crying citizens
as they
march from
heated homes
to freezing
lakes of
tainted hope.

Double Exit Signs

so casually
destructive forces
lead horses
of skeletons
lost in
time abroad
cancel coroners
visits to
the dying
groves of
endless epiphany.

Wooden Fences

Surreptitious ideals
with foggy clouded logic
wind me up like children's
toys
and drive me towards
Death Row.

But this doom
is met with picket
fences
that won't shift or budge
and those fences are
people
holding me up
and back together.

Somehow wooden
fences
keep tanks and inmates
sealed
they avoid breaking
down
though splinter and
fray they must.

Wandering wooden fences
become a holding
force
and I lean all my
weight on them
in case foggy logic
pulls me someplace
else.

The Trees are Budding

The skies are turning
blue
and the grass is growing
green
and although things are crashing
the trees are still budding.

Cameras capture thoughts of
pink
and music hums in
yellow
and despite things falling
the trees are still budding.

Suddenly flowers are
purple
and bonfires glowing
red
disregard the losing battle
the trees are still budding.

So watch the girls in sweaters,
maroon
and their friends in
lavender too
forget that things are not okay
the trees are still budding.

The End

And constant sighs
Conjure lies
So everything you send
To me
Brings forth The End
Of dreams.

Acknowledgements

There are about a million people who deserve to be named in these few lines. To start, my wonderful parents who've been with me since the very literal start, I love you guys. Also, my wonderful sisters. Yes, all three of you. Though we sometimes feel like light years apart, I couldn't ask for better. For my friends, there are too many of you to name without forgetting at least one. Thank you, guys for everything you've done for me whether I've known you for weeks or years. You all put up with a lot of the bad so I'm glad you get to see the good. Finally, thanks to the many English teachers, who, over the years have dealt with pages and pages of writing I've forced you to read and the almost constant question of "Is there a maximum number of words?".

I don't know exactly where myself or this book would be without you all, so this one's for you.

About the author

Born in Ontario, residing in Newfoundland, Sophia Chaffey is a creative marvel. She writes her poetry as commentary on her every day life as a high school student, each piece a snapshot of a moment in time. She is a member of the Beyond the Overpass Youth Theatre program, spending her time creating productions and participating in them in various ways including as an actor, stage manager, set design, props, promotion and more. She is also working on a play. She is an avid reader. Her days are spent maintaining her A+ school grades and working on her artistic interests. She likes black cats and dragons but only one of those is allowed in her bedroom. You may guess which. You can reach her at sophiachaffey@outlook.com

www.ingramcontent.com/pod-product-compliance
Lightning Source LLC
Chambersburg PA
CBHW022049080426
42734CB00009B/1288